HOW TO DRAW
GHOSTS, VAMPIRES & HAUNTED HOUSES

Emma Fischel

Designed by Kim Blundell

Edited by Janet Cook and Anita Ganeri

**Illustrated by Victor Ambrus, Kim Blundell,
Rob McCaig, Mike Pringle and Graham Round**

Contents

SCHOLASTIC INC.

New York   Toronto   London   Auckland   Sydney

About this book

In this book you can see how to draw all kinds of supernatural things. Some are funny, some are mysterious – and some will send shivers down your spine.

Ghosts

On pages 6-13 you can find out how to draw all sorts of different ghosts, for example one that is headless or see-through. Use pages 4-5 to start you off. They show how you can make simple shapes look ghostly by the way you paint them.

These watercolor ghosts are on page 4.

Vampires

Pages 18-21 show you how to draw vampires and all the horrible things associated with them. The picture above of Dracula is on page 21.

Cartoons

There are lots of ideas for funny cartoons in the book, like these cows amazed by the driverless car. On page 19 you can find tips for drawing a cartoon strip.

This cartoon is on page 29.

Haunted houses

You can see how to draw a haunted house on pages 22-23. On pages 24-27 there are all kinds of horrible things you could put inside one, such as the skeleton and spider shown on the left.

Mixing pictures

You could combine different things in the book to make your own ghostly scene. Try drawing a vampire from page 18 creeping through the graveyard on page 16, for example. The haunted house on pages 22-23 would be a good setting for any of the ghosts on pages 6-13. On pages 30-31 there are lots of heads and bodies you could mix to create your own ghost or vampire.

Drawing in stages

Many of the pictures in this book have step-by-step drawing instructions for you to follow. Always copy the outline shapes in pencil. Draw the lines shown in green first, then those shown in red, and lastly the ones shown in blue.

The easiest shapes to draw have one outline.

 ◀ This raven is on page 16.

This genie is on page 9.

More difficult shapes have two outlines.

Make the outlines the size you want your picture to be.

The hardest shapes to draw have three outlines.

See page 14 for how to draw this ghoul.

Pencils

Pencils are marked with a code which tells you how hard or soft they are. Choose a pencil that suits the kind of drawing you want to do. The different pencils you can use are shown below.

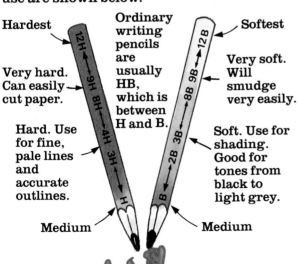

Hardest

Very hard. Can easily cut paper.

Hard. Use for fine, pale lines and accurate outlines.

Ordinary writing pencils are usually HB, which is between H and B.

12H 9H 8H 4H 3H H

Medium

Softest

Very soft. Will smudge very easily.

Soft. Use for shading. Good for tones from black to light grey.

12B 9B 8B 3B 2B B

Medium

Using a fixative spray

Lots of the pictures in this book are drawn with charcoal, chalks or soft pencils. If you use these you then need to use a fixative spray to stop them smudging.

Hold your drawing upright and spray it from about 16 inches away. Use two light coats of spray; one heavy coat will discolor the paper.

This picture is on page 6.

Always use the spray in an open space, preferably outside, as the fumes are dangerous.

Ghostly shapes

What is a ghost? Where do they come from and what do they look like? As no-one really knows, there is no limit to the ways you can draw them. You need to capture the sense of mystery about them because, although people have been telling stories about ghosts for hundreds of years, there is no proof that they even exist.

Here are a few ideas to start you on your way.

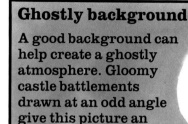

Ghostly background

A good background can help create a ghostly atmosphere. Gloomy castle battlements drawn at an odd angle give this picture an uncomfortable feel.

Shadowy ghosts

To draw these ghosts you will need to use a soft pencil* and thin eraser. First shade all over a sheet of paper with the pencil, then rub out some of the shading to suggest the ghosts' outlines and faces.

Using watercolors

You can use watercolor paints to create the blurred and mysterious look of these ghosts. Follow the steps on the right to draw them.

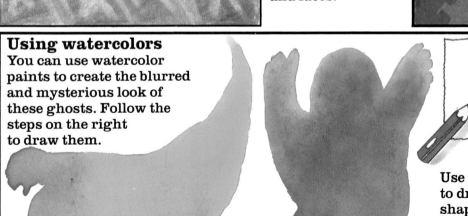

Use faint pencil lines to draw the outline shapes. Make the shapes big so that you have a large surface to paint on.

*See page 3 for the different kinds of pencil you can use.

Use pencil to draw first the ghost shape, then the outline of the castle.

Color the castle with thick felt tips, using diagonal line strokes to fill in the pencil outline. Color the ghost with felt tips and add drooping eyes and a mouth.

First paint the shapes with clean water, then paint streaks of watercolors on top. The paints will blend together, making new colors where they mix.

Cut-out ghosts

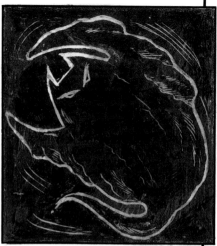

You can use cardboard cut-out shapes to create lots of ghostly effects, like the fiery and devilish ghosts shown above.

To make your cut-out, copy the ghost shape in the pictures above on to a sheet of cardboard and then cut it out with scissors.

Fiery ghost

Put the cut-out on to a smooth surface. Place a sheet of paper over the cut-out.

Rub over the paper with wax crayons, being careful not to move the cut-out.

Color the top part again, so the ghost appears to fade away at the bottom.

Devilish ghost

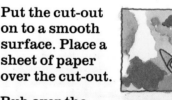

Color a sheet of paper with wax crayons, using lots of different colors.

Cover the whole sheet with a thick layer of black wax crayon.

Create the ghost shape on top by tracing around the cut-out with a dried-up ballpoint pen.

5

Some human ghosts

On these four pages there are lots of human ghosts to draw. Once you have tried them you could use the techniques shown here to make anyone look ghostly. You could turn a pop star or television personality into a see-through ghost, for example, or draw your best friend as a headless ghost . . .

Pirate ghost

There are lots of stories about people who have had violent deaths returning as ghosts. Unable to rest, they are supposed to haunt the scene of their death, like the pirate on the right.

First draw this figure in pencil on a dark sheet of paper. Make it the size you want the finished picture to be.

Draw the lines shown in red. They are the basic shape of the pirate. Erase the lines shown in green.

Draw the lines shown in blue. Go over all the lines with white chalk, then add the shading.*

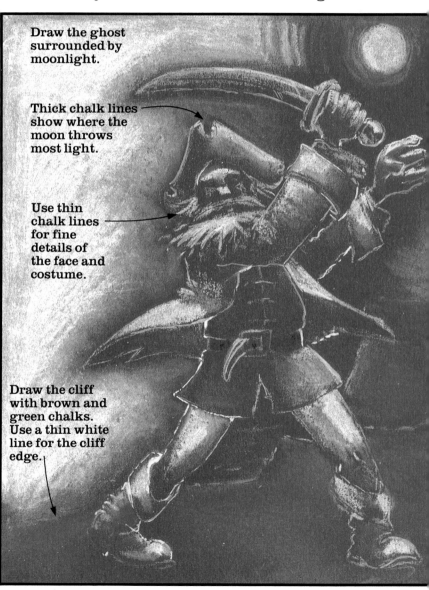

Draw the ghost surrounded by moonlight.

Thick chalk lines show where the moon throws most light.

Use thin chalk lines for fine details of the face and costume.

Draw the cliff with brown and green chalks. Use a thin white line for the cliff edge.

Drawing a sheet ghost

The idea that ghosts are like figures draped in flowing sheets probably came about because the dead used to be buried in white robes, called shrouds.

You can find an easy way to draw a moving sheet ghost below.

Draw the human shape in pencil. Add a sheet around the shape with a felt tip pen. Erase the pencil lines.

Draw thin black lines to show the folds of the sheet. Add a hint of color with a colored pencil.

Draw the bottom of the sheet as a point to make the ghost look as if it is floating. Add eyes and a mouth.

As the ghost moves forwards the head gets bigger. The body narrows into a "V" shape at the bottom.

Seeing a ghost

How would you feel if you saw a ghost? Interested or scared? As a cartoon exaggerates normal features and expressions, it is a good way to draw someone looking very frightened by seeing a ghost. Below are three steps to drawing a cartoon face.

Lines round the face and blobs of sweat show he is quaking with fear.

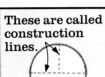

These are called construction lines.

Draw a circle with two pencil lines crossing it.

Eyes equal distances from nose.

Ears level with nose.

Draw the nose where the lines meet. Add the eyes and ears.

Drooping mouth

Erase the pencil lines and add hair and a mouth.

By making a few changes to the basic cartoon face on the left you can show someone looking really terrified.

Headless ghost

The headless ghost of Anne Boleyn, second wife of Henry VIII of England, is said to haunt Hampton Court in London. To draw her ghost, first copy the outlines below on to black paper. Make your outline the size you want the finished picture to be.

Use pencil for the outlines.

Erase the green lines.

Anne Boleyn was beheaded in 1536.

Paint the ghost with white watercolor.* You will need a thick and a thin brush.

Paint the outline and fine details, like the lace, with a thin, wet brush.

Use a thick brush for the folds of material. The brush should be dry and the paint so thick that it will almost not leave the brush.

Put your ghost in a setting such as the doorway shown here.

Doppelganger

This ghost is called a doppelganger. It is the double of a living person.

Paint a face on one half of a sheet of paper. Fold the paper in half. Press the sides together then open them up again.

Use thick, dry paint.

See-through ghosts

A ghost may appear to glide through solid objects. To get a see-through effect you can use watercolors on top of wax. As they don't mix, anything drawn in wax will show through watercolors.

Follow these steps to draw this picture.

1. Draw the background shapes in pencil.

2. Draw the ghosts with thin wax crayons.

You could also use white poster paint.

Genie

The story of Aladdin and his magic lamp is well known. Every time he rubs the lamp a genie rises out of it in a puff of smoke and grants him a wish.

Use the shapes below to draw the genie.

Thread spool

Draw this outline very big so that you can decorate the costume in some of the ways shown here.

Draw in the details of the face, hands and costume. Add smoke shapes around the outline.

Paint the costume with pale watercolors. Let the paint dry before you decorate the costume.

Toothpaste lid

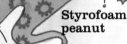
Styrofoam peanut

3. Now paint a thin layer of water over the whole picture, then paint streaks of pale watercolors on it while the paper is still wet.

4. Once the paint is dry, go over the pencil lines with a thin black felt tip pen.

Printing

You could make patterns on the costume by dipping any of the things shown above into paint or ink, then pressing them on to the picture.

You could also use potato prints. First cut a potato in half and cut shapes into the flat edge.* Then use the cut edge to make patterns.

*Always cut away from your hand so that you don't cut yourself if the knife slips.

Ghosts from around the world

Every country has its own ghost stories and legends. Here you can see just some of the strange ghosts to be found around the world.

Ghost from Ancient China

In Ancient China, murdered people were said to return as ghosts, appearing from a shapeless cloud and surrounded by green light.

To draw this picture first copy the outlines below. Go over the finished outline with thin green and black ballpoint pens.

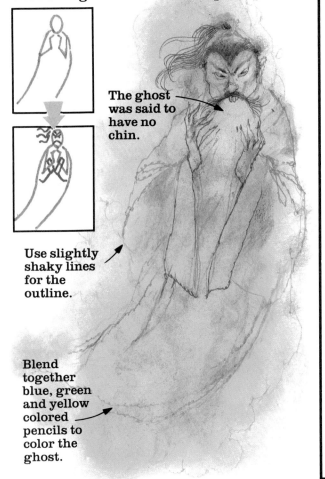

The ghost was said to have no chin.

Use slightly shaky lines for the outline.

Blend together blue, green and yellow colored pencils to color the ghost.

Japanese ghost

Use a black felt tip pen to go over the outline.

The Ancient Japanese believed that people who had led evil lives came back as ghosts. As a punishment for their wickedness, their legs were always in flames.

Use the outlines below to help you draw this ghost, then color it in with felt tips.

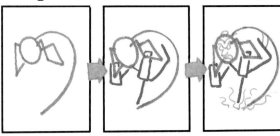

Scottish kelpie

This ghost is called a kelpie. You could copy or trace the picture, then color it with colored pencils. Use black and purple to draw the outline, and to add details to the face and coat. Use a mixture of colors to shade over the top.

According to Scottish legend, kelpies persuaded unwary travellers to ride them across a river. Once on a kelpie's back, travellers were unable to get off and the kelpie drowned them.

Use long lines for the tail and mane.

Dark shading shows the muscles.

Seeing this dog is supposed to mean certain death.

Phantom hound

This phantom dog, called Barquest, is said to be found near graveyards in France. Use the outline below to draw it, then color the ghost with black felt tip. Use short, wavy lines to show its shaggy fur.

Egyptian khu

This Ancient Egyptian ghost is called a khu. People believed it caused diseases in human beings and drove animals mad. You can see how to draw it below.

Outline the eyes and beak in black.

First paint a watercolor wash over the paper.* Let it dry, then copy the outlines above in pencil. Draw in the background with fine felt tips and color the ghost with red felt tip.

*See the see-through ghosts on page 8 for how to paint a watercolor wash.

Ghostly vehicles

Not all ghosts are of people or animals. A ghostly vehicle may haunt the route of its last journey, replaying the moments of a fatal crash.

Drawing a ghost train

Copy the shape below to draw this ghost train. First draw the green lines to help you get the proportions of the train right. The carriages look smaller as they get further away; this is called perspective.
Use pastel pencils to color the train.* Start by using black pastel to define the edges of the train then build up the other colors.

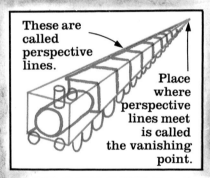

These are called perspective lines.

Place where perspective lines meet is called the vanishing point.

Add steam with white pastel.

Smooth in color by rubbing it with a soft rag.

Yellow and white shading shows where lightning highlights part of the train.

White lines give impression of speed.

Draw rails with black and purple line strokes.

Ghostly fact

In 1879, a Scottish night train plunged off a bridge whose middle section had blown away. It was rebuilt but years later a silent train was seen rushing over it, vanishing where the bridge had collapsed.

*Prevent smudging with a fixative spray (see page 3).

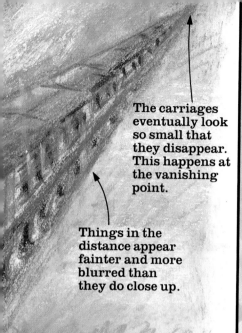

The carriages eventually look so small that they disappear. This happens at the vanishing point.

Things in the distance appear fainter and more blurred than they do close up.

Phantom ship

To draw this ship, first dampen a sheet of paper with water. Dab runny poster or powder paints on to the sheet with a brush. The colors will spread on the wet paper.

Once the paint is dry, draw the ship with grey felt tip. Add foam by dabbing thick white paint round the ship with a rag or tissue.

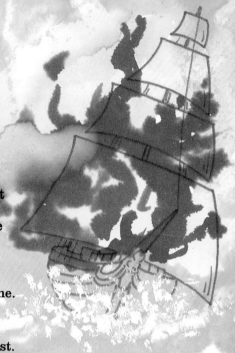

This is the ghost of The Palatine. It was looted and set on fire in 1752. Each anniversary its blazing ghost is said to sail along the North American coast.

Drawing your own ghostly vehicle

Now try creating your own ghostly truck, based on the outline on the right. First, follow the grid method shown below to make the truck the size you want your finished picture to be.

You can use a grid to enlarge or reduce the size of any picture. Draw a grid on tracing paper. Tape it over the picture then follow the steps for drawing the truck.

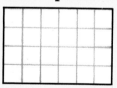

Draw a grid with the same number of squares as the truck grid. The size of your truck will depend on how big the squares are.

Look at the shape in each square of the truck grid. Copy it on to the same square in your grid. Rub out the grid lines.

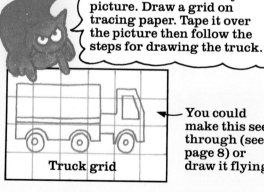

Truck grid

You could make this see-through (see page 8) or draw it flying.

You can adapt the grid method to draw any vehicle you like. How about a phantom tractor, cruise ship, car, rocket, or even a UFO?

Ghost train ride

A ride on a ghost train can be a terrifying experience. Once the train moves into the tunnel there is only one way out: forward . . .

On these pages you can see how to draw just some of the ghastly things that might be lurking round the next bend in the track.

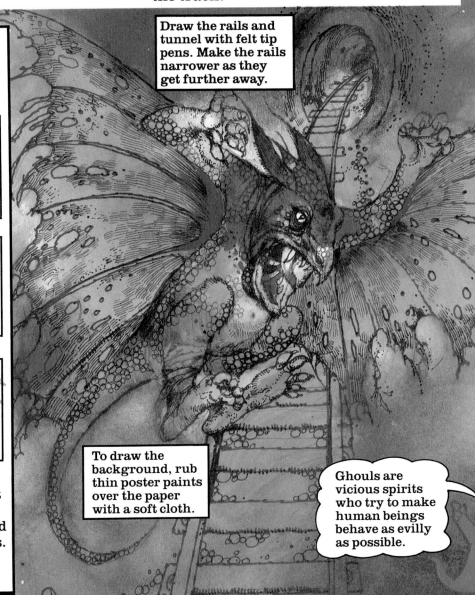

Gruesome ghoul

To draw this ghoul, first copy the outlines below in pencil.

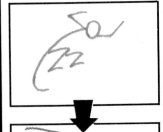

Go round the outline with a black ballpoint pen and add details like the scaly skin and shading on the wings. Color the ghoul with felt tips.

Draw the rails and tunnel with felt tip pens. Make the rails narrower as they get further away.

To draw the background, rub thin poster paints over the paper with a soft cloth.

Ghouls are vicious spirits who try to make human beings behave as evilly as possible.

Grinning skull

To draw this skull, first copy or trace the picture. Go round the outline in black and color it in with felt tips.

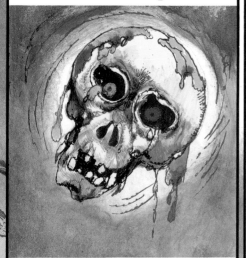

Color the yellow areas, then add green and orange on top. Use bright colors for the slime and eyes. Fill in the black areas and add fine details with red and black ballpoint pens.

Ghostly fiend

This hideous fiend is drawn using watercolors, ballpoint pens and colored pencils.

First paint a thin layer of pale green watercolor over the page. Once the paint is dry, copy the outline shapes below on to the paint using faint pencil lines.

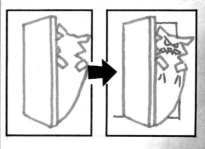

Copy details of the face and doorway from the main picture, using black, green and red ballpoint pens. Shade the doorway and the fiend's clothes with green and black colored pencils.

Cobwebs

To draw a cobweb on the wall of your tunnel, first copy the outline on the right. Draw over it with a black ballpoint pen, using shaky line strokes to suggest that the web is quite fragile.

Add a black spider crawling out from the middle of its web.

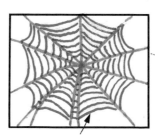

Continue drawing the lines shown in red until your cobweb is the size you want.

Graveyards

Graveyards are quiet and mysterious places, full of strange shapes and dark trees, with a history that may go back hundreds of years.

These pages show you how to draw a graveyard and the things you might expect to find in it – as well as some you might hope not to.

Drawing the graveyard

The shapes of things in the graveyard are quite simple to draw. It is the way they are colored that creates the atmosphere.

This picture was colored with colored pencils. On the opposite page you will find lots of tips on shading with crayons to get different effects.

Erase a curved shape, then draw in the bats.

The raven is said to be a herald of death.

Draw pale, slanting lines to give the graveyard a misty look.

This is the Graveyard Guardian, the spirit of the first person buried in the graveyard. It returns to protect the other graves from evil.

Raven

Use the outline above to help you draw this raven. Color it with black colored pencil, using short line strokes to show its ragged feathers. Use darker shading under the body to show its rounded shape.

To give the stone a textured look, put sandpaper under the page when you color the tomb.

Draw shadows with purple and black crayons.

Use blue and green colored pencils to draw in yew trees, which are always found in graveyards.

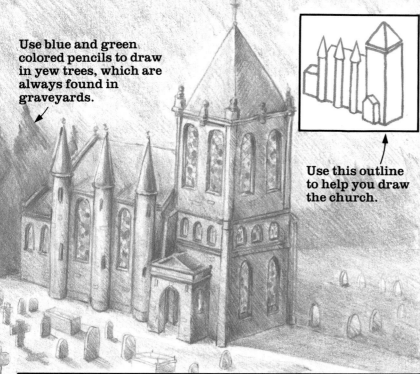

Use this outline to help you draw the church.

Stained glass window

Follow the stages below to draw the stained glass windows on the church.

First, draw the arch shape in pencil and a line of the pattern down the middle of the window. Next, build up the shapes on either side.

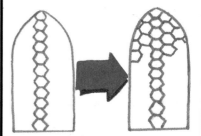

Go over the outlines with a thin black pen and color the shapes with felt tips.

Add extra lines to simple shapes.

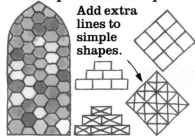

Above you can also see suggestions for different patterns you could use.

Graveyard Guardian

To draw the Graveyard Guardian, start with the outlines on the right. Color it in with colored pencils, using blue and grey for the folds of the robe and darker colors inside the hood.

A Graveyard Guardian has no face.

Technique tips

Below you can see the different shading methods used in the main picture.*

 Hatching

 Cross-hatching

 Stippling

 Texturing

 Smudging

 Erasing

*See page 3 for the different kinds of pencil you can use.

Vampires

Vampires are said to be living corpses who feed on human blood. They leave the grave at sunset in search of human victims. These pages show some of the strange ways a vampire might behave. There could be many more . . .

Drawing a cartoon vampire

To draw this cartoon vampire, first copy the figures below.

Add a shadow.

Draw deadly fangs for piercing victims' necks.

Copy the figure shown in green to get the proportions of the body right. Draw the cloak around the body and add details to the face. Color the vampire with felt tips.

Moving vampires

Use the green figures to help you draw these moving vampires. Fill in the body shapes around the figures.

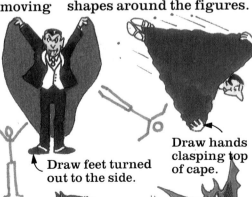

Draw right leg bent back and left arm round face.

Draw feet turned out to the side.

Draw hands clasping top of cape.

Vampire victim

A vampire hypnotizes its victims so that they do not struggle and will remember nothing of the attack.

Use the outlines below to help you draw this vampire victim. As she is looking to one side, the position of her features is different from the cartoon face on page 7.

Vertical construction line is curved.

Line across stays the same.

Eyes move round.

Ears move so only one shows.

Nose moves to where lines meet.

Vampires return night after night until their victims die. Then they too become vampires.

Vampire cartoon strip

Artists use lots of ways to make cartoon strips look interesting and funny. Below are some professional tips which you could use to create your own vampire cartoon strip.

Short piece of text sets time and place.

Jagged edge to speech bubble suggests a ringing sound.

Shape of letters can help to emphasize the word.

Put bubbles over uncluttered areas.

It is mainly the pictures that tell the story, not the text.

A vampire has no reflection in a mirror.

MIDNIGHT IN THE VAMPIRE FAMILY HOME...

ZZZZZ Z ZZZZZZZZZZZ

RRING RRING

YAWN!

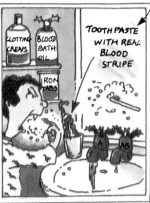

CLOTTING CREAM

BLOOD BATH OIL

IRON TABS

TOOTH PASTE WITH REAL BLOOD STRIPE

BREAKFAST TIME!

BLOOD ORANGES

AB

HOW ABOUT SOME TV BEFORE WE GO TO WORK?

YIPPEE!

AND NOW FOR OUR LATE NIGHT FILM — "THE HOUSE OF BLOOD"

OH, NO! NOT ANOTHER FAMILY VIDEO!

Use unusual viewpoints.

Conversation starts here as people read from left to right.

Vary close-ups and longer views.

Different size frames add interest.

Strip should end with a strong punch-line.

Other vampire characters

Here are some suggestions for other characters you could use in your vampire cartoon strip.

Baby Vamp

Fang the spider

Granny Vamp and Tibbles

Drawing a werewolf

Werewolves are human beings who change into savage, wolf-like creatures when there is a full moon. They live on human flesh and can only be killed by a silver bullet or knife. They have to be burnt when they die. If they are buried they become vampires.

To draw this werewolf, first copy these outlines.

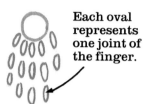

Use thin black felt tip to draw his hair. Outline his features, then draw wrinkled skin using short felt tip line strokes. Color the whole picture with colored pencils.

Vampire hands

Vampire hands are very thin and bony. Hands are difficult to draw, so use the steps below to help you.

Each oval represents one joint of the finger.

Draw green veins.

Erase the ovals before adding details.

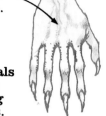

First, draw the hand as a series of oval shapes.

Next, draw the hand outline round the ovals.

Add details like the nails and knuckles.

More hands to draw

Here are some suggestions for drawing vampire hands in other positions.

Hands are about as long as the distance from a person's chin to their hairline.

Bats

Vampires can turn themselves into bats to fly through windows and attack their sleeping victims.

These bats are drawn with black and red felt tip pens. Use the outlines to help you draw them.

Add eyes and a mouth.

Dracula

The most famous vampire of all is the evil Count Dracula. He first appeared as a character in a book by Bram Stoker in 1897.

Here Dracula is about to carry out one of his ghastly attacks. Try tracing this picture, then use the tips below to color it.

Use this outline to help you draw the part of the cloak hidden by the parchment.

1. Color the outside of his cloak, his hair and bow tie with black poster paint. Use red on the inside of his cloak and top of his waistcoat, then add the red details to his mouth and round his eyes. Paint his trousers grey. Let this dry, then add black stripes.

2. Color his skin and waistcoat with colored pencils.

3. Use short, fine lines of green and black ballpoint pen to add further shading to his clothes and skin, then draw the pattern round the top of his waistcoat.

Story of Dracula

In Bram Stoker's story, Dracula lived in a huge rambling castle in Transylvania in eastern Europe. He wanted to fill the world with vampires and planned to start in England. He travelled there by ship, killing all the crew and drinking their blood. He terrorized London with a wave of vampire attacks but was chased back to Transylvania and killed by a knife being stabbed through his heart.

Haunted houses

Everyone knows what makes a house look haunted – or do they? How do you draw echoing footsteps, strange noises or sudden icy drafts?

Here are some ideas for ways to create a menacing atmosphere and suggest an unseen ghostly presence.

Drawing the picture

To draw the picture on the right, first paint the sky across the whole page. You can see how to draw it and the rest of the background on the opposite page. Once the sky is dry draw the house on top, using the shapes below to help. Paint the house following the tips below, then add the trees and other details.

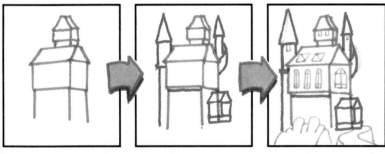

Painting the house

The picture is painted in gouache, a form of watercolor professional artists often use. Its advantage over ordinary watercolors is that light colors can be painted on top of dark ones. If you don't have gouache, you could use poster paints.

The house casts lots of strange and sinister shadows. To paint them, first copy the dark areas on the left in pencil.

Now fill them in with black poster paint. Let the paint dry then paint the rest of the shape mid-grey. You can see how to add more detail on the opposite page.

Adding detail

The main types of brickwork are shown on the right. Use quite thick poster paint for them, so that they show up well. Make sure the original layer of grey paint is dry before you start.

White oblongs

Grey oblongs

White lines

Grey lines

Copy the picture for more detailed shading, like that on the windows. Use pale blue to highlight parts of the house not in direct moonlight. Draw trailing plants with strokes of green paint, and add a light in the window with yellow paint.

Drawing the background

The background plays a large part in creating the ghostly effect of this picture. Below are some tips to help you draw it.

Use wavy lines of brown paint for the tree. Let it dry and add white highlights. Draw the flying leaves with blobs of brown and yellow paint. ▶

◀ Paint the sky dark blue. Add other shades on top, letting each color dry before you add the next. Draw the rain with white chalk lines once the picture is completed.

You can see how to draw bats on page 20.

Inside the house

The rooms inside a haunted house may have been kept locked for hundreds of years, left exactly as they were after some terrible tragedy.

Here, the outer wall has been cut away to show the inside of the haunted house. Use ideas from this picture to create your own haunted room. On the next two pages you can see how to draw some of the strange things in this picture.

Adding interest

A haunted room will look more interesting if you draw the main objects in unusual positions or at unexpected angles. Put objects of different shapes and heights near each other to add variety.

Decide where the light is coming from before you start to draw. Then you can use it to create a ghostly atmosphere, by drawing lots of shadows, for example.

A cat senses a strange atmosphere and hisses for no apparent reason.

Light from the moon reveals a trapdoor in the floor.

A grandfather clock chiming thirteen means there will soon be a death in the family.

Years of neglect have caused cracks and cobwebs.

Bloodstains cannot be removed, no matter how much they are scrubbed.

Drawing in the floorboard lines gives a three-dimensional feel to the picture.

Poltergeists

Poltergeists are invisible spirits who cause chaos in a house by seeming to give objects a life of their own.

You cannot see poltergeists but you can certainly see their effects. Furniture flies across a room and smashes to pieces, objects appear from nowhere, mirrors break or musical instruments start to play by themselves.

Ghostly breezes make the curtains sway, although there is no draft in the room.

The skeleton of a forgotten prisoner is slumped in the corner of a torture chamber.

You can see how to draw this skeleton on the next page.

Poltergeist is a German word. It means noisy spirit.

Moving the front of the fake fireplace reveals a secret door.

A secret room is used to hide from enemies. It is reached by stairs hidden behind the fake fireplace.

A 17th century cavalier steps out of his portrait. Cavaliers supported King Charles I of England, but were defeated in the civil war which caused his downfall. Many cavaliers were executed with the king.

Echoing footsteps can be heard and ghostly prints appear as if from nowhere.

Ghostly fact

An ancient story tells of a woman who wanted her skull built into a wall of her house when she died, but, despite her wishes, she was buried in the family vault. Immediately afterwards, loud crashing noises, groans and slamming doors were heard. The family decided to do what she asked. The skull was built into a wall and there was peace again.

Skeleton

To draw this skeleton, first copy the outlines shown below it. Draw round the finished outline with black felt tip. Color the bones with a mixture of pale blue and grey watercolors.

An adult skeleton has 206 bones. These are the main ones.

The ribs gradually get narrower.

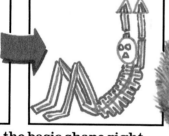

Once you have got the basic shape right, you could try drawing your skeleton in different poses, like the three below.

Sad skeleton

Pouncing skeleton

Dancing skeleton

Cats and rats...

You could draw the cat below hissing at an empty chair, or the rat gnawing on a piece of moldy food.

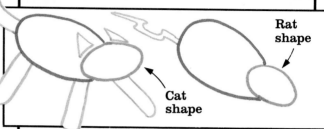

Rat shape

Cat shape

Drawing fur

To draw fur, first paint a thin wash of watercolor over the body. When it is dry, draw lots of colored pencil lines over the top.

Draw sharp front teeth and evil red eyes.

Add a shadow under the body.

Draw the ears bent right back.

Draw the whiskers sticking straight out.

Leave the paws white.

...and spiders

To draw this spider, first pencil in a circle for the head and a larger oval shape for the body. Add eight legs and color the spider with colored pencils.

Short lines round the outline make it look hairy.

Portrait ghost

You could copy or trace this portrait ghost or, if you want to make your picture bigger than this, use a grid.* Color the ghost with a mixture of watercolors and colored pencils.

Use fine shading lines on his face.

Paint the picture frame yellow, then add patterns with colored pencils.

Grandfather clock

Draw the basic shapes of this clock in pencil. Color with colored pencils to suggest the texture and patterns in the wood, using shades of light and dark brown.

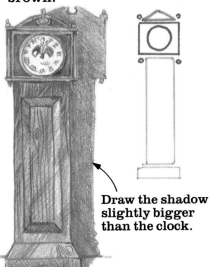

Draw the shadow slightly bigger than the clock.

Texture

Use three shades of watercolor to paint the ghost's jacket and trousers.

First paint a thin wash with the lightest shade.

Let it dry, then paint the middle shade on top, leaving some parts pale.

Use the dark shade to paint areas of shadow.

Pale areas suggest the soft material.

Paint the boots with pale brown watercolor. Let it dry, then shade with a dark colored pencil.

*See page 13 for how to use a grid.

Drawing the unexpected

One way of suggesting that a ghost may be present is by drawing ordinary objects doing something completely unexpected. These pages show you how to draw things that could never possibly happen – or could they?

Floating table

To draw a picture of a floating table, you need to put it on a background which shows that the table is up in the air.

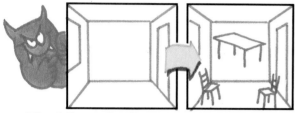

First draw the floor and walls, then the door and window. Make your picture large to leave room for the furniture.

Draw the table and chairs and rub out the background lines behind them. Add details from the main picture.

Color the picture with colored pencils. →

Add shadows underneath the furniture.

Ghostly shadows

You can get really funny effects by giving a shadow its own identity, separate from the person or object it belongs to. Try copying the ones below, then think up some shadow pictures of your own. You could make a shadow dance or draw a spiky plant shadow, for example.

Draw in the floor line. ↙

Use solid blocks of color to fill in the shadows.

Draw a mantelpiece under the clock.

This shadow has become a ghostly monster.

Vanishing kettle

To draw these pictures of a kettle gradually being swallowed up by its own steam, first copy the three kettle shapes in pencil. Sketch in the steam, making it bigger at each stage.

Use charcoal to fill in the outlines, smudging it with your finger to get the rounded shapes of the kettle and steam.* Add eyes and a gaping mouth to the steam.

Areas left white give the kettle a metallic shine.

Crazy cartoons

The piano and car in these cartoons seem to have a life of their own – or is some strange invisible presence at work? Use the shapes below to help you draw them.

Now add detail to the outline shapes, using the finished pictures as guides. Color your pictures, using darker felt tip pens to outline the shapes and paler ones inside.

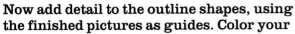

*Use a fixative spray to stop the picture smudging (see page 3).

Mix and match

Here are lots of suggestions for different parts of ghost and vampire bodies. You can mix them in any combination for really peculiar results.

Try drawing a tiptoeing vampire with a chuckling ghost's head or an angry ghost with knocking knees, for example.

Sheet ghosts

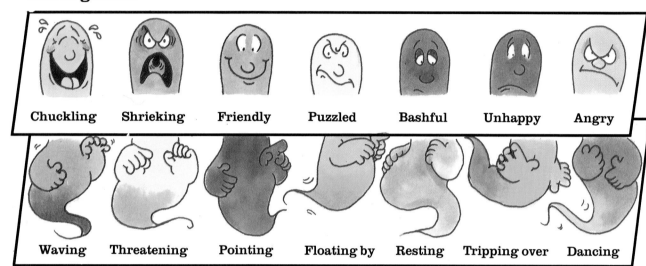

| Chuckling | Shrieking | Friendly | Puzzled | Bashful | Unhappy | Angry |

| Waving | Threatening | Pointing | Floating by | Resting | Tripping over | Dancing |

Vampires

| Sly | Thirsty | Gleeful | Angry | Tired | Thoughtful | Shifty |

| Tiptoeing | Creeping | Climbing | Jumping | Crawling | Swooping | Lurking |

Seeing ghosts

Shocked · Anxious · Puzzled · Alarmed · Sickly · Petrified · Disappearing fast

Wringing hands · Fingers crossed · Pointing · Walking · Tripping over · Running · Quick getaway

Standing · Climbing · Knees knocking · Walking · Tripping over · Running · Help!

Things to add

Sinister butler · Crazy clock · Bone china · Night watchman · Bone chair · Talking heads · Deadly duo · Creepy crawly · Bat walking stick

Index

ISBN 0-590-92189-4

Copyright © 1988 by Usborne Publishing Ltd.
All rights reserved. Published by Scholastic Inc., 555 Broadway, New York, NY 10012, by arrangement with Usborne Publishing Ltd.

12 11 10 9 8 7 6 5 4 3 2 1

6 7 8 9/9 0 1/0
23

Printed in the U.S.A.
First Scholastic printing, September 1996